Money Moves

Five Money Moves the Average American
Should Know to Win with Money and Avoid
Financial Catastrophe

Lucas de Brito, MBA

Copyright © 2020 Lucas de Brito.

All rights reserved. No part of this publication may be reproduced, distributed, or transmitted in any form or by any means, including photocopying, recording, or other electronic or mechanical methods, without the prior written permission of the publisher, except in the case of brief quotations embodied in reviews and certain other non-commercial uses permitted by copyright law.

ISBN: 978-0-578-71828-6

Editing by William Croyle

Cover design by dezinir.99

Cover image ©Adobe Stock ID 311159270 Author ©300_librarians Extended License

DISCLAIMER

All information provided in this book is the author's opinion and does not constitute any financial, legal, or any other type of advice. If financial, legal, or any other type of advice is needed, the reader should seek guidance from a qualified professional who can discuss individual needs. The author does not make representations as to accuracy, completeness, suitability, or validity of any information in this book and will not be liable for any errors or omissions in this information or any losses or damages arising from its use. The author does not make any personal investments on behalf of the reader, nor does he provide specific investment advice. The reader may not consider any examples, documents, or other content in the book or otherwise provided by the author to be the equivalent of professional advice.

DEDICATION

My dear family,
Thank you for providing meaning to my life
and for showing me that true love exists.
I wrote this book for you.

CONTENTS

	Acknowledgments	i
1	Introduction	1
2	Move 1: Digitize & Visualize Your Money	Pg 5
3	Move 2: Get Your Priorities Right	Pg 13
4	Move 3: Shrink Today & Expand Your Tomorrow	Pg 31
5	Move 4: Invest Now for Your Future	Pg 45
6	Move 5: Have a Long-term Growth Action Plan	Pg 65
7	Index	Pg 75
8	About the Author	Pg 77

ACKNOWLEDGMENTS

Thank you to my wife
for sharing with me the joys and challenges
of raising two small children.
Life would not be possible without you.

INTRODUCTION

> "Someone is sitting in the shade today because someone planted a tree a long time ago."
>
> Warren Buffett

I believe all adults should strive to become financially literate and competent with their money. The implications of mishandling money can be catastrophic for multiple generations. Money doesn't buy happiness, but it does give you options, including living in a safer neighborhood, attending a better school, seeking appropriate medical care, eating healthy, traveling the world, and sleeping better at night.

Unfortunately, the education system does a poor job teaching young adults how to manage their finances. In this book, you will learn the financial moves I've used to win with money, regardless of what is happening in the world. I began my financial journey at the end of the last Great Recession, and I finished writing this book during the Covid-19 pandemic. I have fared quite well financially in times of crisis. Some may argue I'm even thriving.

This book is not for the seasoned investor. It is for those who are delving into the financial world for the first time, specifically young people such as college graduates, newlyweds, and new parents. The content, both educational and practical, will give you the foundation you need to begin improving your financial status immediately.

Though I have a bachelor's degree in economics and an MBA, the practical knowledge I will share with you is largely based on more than a decade of personal research and experience that have nothing to do with my degrees. In fact, earning the degrees is what initially put me in debt, which motivated me to learn how to take control of my present and future finances.

I immigrated to the United States from Brazil at the age of 17 to attend college. Because my family lived outside of the U.S., I had to learn everything from opening a bank account to paying bills to managing a credit card all on my own. I was more than $30,000 in debt upon finishing my MBA and needed to get a hold of my finances sooner rather than later. I was disappointed at how little I had been taught about personal finances in college, so I began to read books on my own. Considering that most Americans live paycheck to paycheck regardless of their income, I learned that personal finances had a lot more to do with behavior and mindset rather than the rate of return of an investment. Therefore, I will not get into the complicated specifics of how a stock is valued or how bonds behave in relation to interest rates. I simply want to motivate you to dig yourself out of debt and/or start saving money for your retirement and investments. I want to put you on the road to wealth and financial security.

The five chapters you will read feature the same steps that I have taken to achieve my success. I still recommend you apply your own thinking and decide for yourself the best course of action for your situation. You should seek a competent financial professional if you feel you need one. My goal is to introduce you to some ideas and support your decision making. At the end of each chapter are key action items for you to review. I also provide you with a link for additional resources you can browse and review. If you are married, I recommend you and your spouse work through your finances together as a team.

Managing your finances does not have to be stressful. The more you know, the more enjoyable the journey can be.

BE ORGANIZED WITH YOUR MONEY

MOVE 1:
DIGITIZE AND VISUALIZE YOUR MONEY

"In the land of the blind, the one-eyed man is king."

Desiderius Erasmus

You can't manage what you don't measure. It is far too common for people to not have a clear picture of what is happening to their money. They simply don't know where it is or where it went. This lack of visibility creates a situation in which it is extremely difficult for a person to win with money.

Let's use a health analogy to understand this further. If you were unhappy with your weight, one of the first steps you'd take would be to get on a scale to find out your current weight. Being able to visualize what today looks like makes you better equipped to determine how tomorrow should be. Once you have that number, you would figure out how much weight you want to lose and formulate a plan of action to lose it, such as eating healthier and exercising more. After you execute that plan for a week through a lot of hard work, you step on the scale to see the results of your efforts represented by a lower number than what you saw the previous week. That's what winning looks like, and it will motivate you to keep going. We will use a similar approach to improve your financial health.

The first action you will take today is to see an overall picture of your financial condition through the use of an online financial platform. Many online platforms allow you to connect your entire financial picture into one place either free of charge or for a very little cost. These platforms allow you to centralize information about your bank accounts, credit cards, loans, investments, and other property you may have in an automated manner. Think of these platforms as the equivalent of the scale in my weight-loss analogy.

I've used an online platform called Mint for several years. It not only organizes my finances, but it also allows me to budget my money, set goals, and monitor my credit score. While Mint has worked well for me, other platforms you can consider include Personal Capital and You Need a Budget (YNAB). Research them and pick one that is best for you.

Please note that these platforms will gain read access to your accounts. While the risk of being hacked always exists anytime technology is used, I have never had an issue.

To get started, pick a platform and sign up, then proceed to sync up to your bank accounts, retirement accounts, credit card accounts, mortgages, vehicles, student loans, cryptocurrency, and whatever else you have today. Create a user-defined account so that you can manually enter information in the event one of the accounts you have is unable to connect to the platform. After you've finished entering all your relevant financial information, the system will automatically classify your transactions into different categories such as income, home expense, transportation expense, food and dining expense, education expense, etc. This classification is helpful but can sometimes be incorrect (i.e., a restaurant bill may be classified under health care instead of food and dining). Go through the list of transactions for the previous and current months and correct any mistakes you see in the classification.

Believe it or not, that's all there is to it. You have just taken a giant first step in your journey toward financial freedom. Digitizing your finances eliminates the time burden of doing things the old fashioned way. Without much effort, you've organized your financial data into one place, and it is accessible from virtually any device with internet access.

Additionally, most of these platforms have a corresponding App you can download to a mobile device (typically free of charge) if you'd like to track your finances through your phone.

You will notice on your platform a couple of key financial indicators (KFIs) summarized in a dashboard format based on the financial data you provided. These indicators are net worth and net income, both fundamental metrics of your financial health you will use going forward as a compass of your progress. Going back to the weight loss example, if the online platform is the scale of your financial life, then net worth and net income are the displays of your financial weight.

Net worth is a snapshot capturing the sum of everything you own (assets) minus everything that you owe (liabilities, or debts). The report that lists your assets and liabilities is called your personal balance sheet. The net worth number may be positive, negative, or zero. For example, if on January 31 you have $500 in your bank account and you own a vehicle worth $10,000, your assets are $10,500. If you also have $10,000 in student loans on January 31, your net worth that day is $500 ($10,500 in assets minus $10,000 in liabilities). Net worth is your total wealth. Your goal is to increase this number over time by owning more assets like cash, properties, stocks, etc. as opposed to having debts like car loans, student loans, or credit card balances.

The next KFI you must know is your net income. Net income shows the difference between how much you earned versus how much you spent over a specific time. For example, if in February you earned $4,000, and your expenses with rent, food, transportation, student loans, etc. were $3,500, your net income for February would be $500. If your net income is positive, you are adding to your net worth as you have more assets. If it is negative, you are most likely reducing your net worth. Do you see how net worth and net income work together? These two KFIs allow you to keep track of your financial progress and enable you to set meaningful and measurable goals.

Now that you understand net worth and net income a little more, let's identify your net worth and net income. First, what is your current net worth? You may be able to quickly answer this question already with the online financial dashboard that has been created for you. In any case, use a piece of paper or a spreadsheet to list all your assets and debts from highest to lowest. Also, write down the amount of interest you are paying on each debt item (you will use this in the future). Once complete, add all your assets and subtract all your debts to get your net worth. Next, what is your net income for this month and last month? Once again, this exercise may be completed already if you categorized your expenses correctly in the online financial platform you signed up for. If not, write down for each month your total income and subtract your expenses to get your net income for each month. Please proceed only after you are done figuring out your net worth and net income (two months), and listing your debts from top to bottom with their interest rates.

Now that you can see your current financial condition, there is a third KFI I'd like for you to become familiar with to establish a comprehensive baseline of your financial health: your credit score. Your credit score is a number that typically varies from 300 to 850 and is supposed to tell a creditor (someone who extends you credit) what your creditworthiness is. It demonstrates how well you've been able to manage your debts over time. Your credit score factors in items such as the length of your credit history, on-time payments, number of accounts, the amount owed, and type of debt. A higher credit score can be beneficial as it may give you lower interest rates on loans, or perhaps a smaller deposit requirement if you are renting an apartment. Occasionally, there are errors or perhaps fraudulent activities that may hurt your credit score. You must identify any issues and work to correct them. Your next task is to learn your current credit score (if any) and if there are any errors associated with your name. The three reporting agencies that provide a credit score are TransUnion, Experian, and

Equifax. You may need to reach out to them individually to fix any mistakes. Go to www.annualcreditreport.com to get your free credit reports from each agency. Note that the online financial platform you've signed up for may already provide you with some visibility to your credit score from one or more agencies. Check for any updates to your credit score once a month and see how you're tracking. Furthermore, you can download free Apps such as Credit Karma or Credit Sesame which provide credit monitoring capabilities.

MOVE 1: DIGITIZE & VISUALIZE YOUR MONEY

Key Action Items

Visit **rebrand.ly/MoneyMoves** for more resources.

1. Sign up with an online platform, sync up all relevant financial accounts, and fix any errors with the classification of past transactions (two months history). Optional: download a mobile app if available.
2. Find out your current net worth and net income for the past two months.
3. List your debts highest to lowest with interest rates and balance amounts. Add them up.
4. Find out your current credit score. Get your three credit reports and watch for errors. Optional: download a free credit monitoring App.

Once you have done all of this and understand the concepts of net worth, net income, and credit score, you are ready to proceed to the next chapter.

MOVE 2:
GET YOUR PRIORITIES RIGHT

"Don't tell me where your priorities are. Show me where you spend your money and I'll tell you what they are."

James W. Frick

The three KFIs provide you with insightful metrics you should consult periodically to keep track of your progress. Awareness is a great first step toward winning with your finances. But now that you can measure your money, what do you do with it?

You need to manage it in a positive way.

In this chapter, I share my views on how to prioritize your

money so that you get the most protection and benefit from it. Essentially, before I tell you to budget and eat cheap noodles for six months, I want you to have a clear perspective on the milestones you should chase.

The first point, protection, is all about developing a money shield. A money shield is a term I use to describe a fully-funded emergency fund. I will use both terms interchangeably.

The second point, benefit, is all about investments. I think of investments as a spear helping you hunt and gather more resources for your financial house that will eventually lead to retirement.

I strongly believe the order you go about it is key. If you were building a house, you wouldn't build the roof first before you build the foundation. But what about debt? Debt creates risk and works against you; therefore, you will work on eliminating it. Getting out of debt will fall in between fully funding your money shield and ramping up your investments. More to come on this. First, I will summarize the pecking order you should use when structuring your financial house.

If you have debt:

Priority 1: Build a 1-month money shield to cover the 4 financial walls (food, access to basic home utilities like electricity and water, a roof over your head, and access to transportation) plus insurance.

Priority 2: Get rid of debts, except for home (if you own).
- Tackle the debt by boosting your income and by reducing your monthly expenses.
- Pause investments up to 2 years until you're out of debt. If your employer offers a retirement account with matching contributions, then it's okay to contribute to get the match.
- Prioritize paying the IRS first since they could send you to prison (not a joke). Make sure you continue making your mortgage payments. Get fired up about getting rid of all your other debts such as student loans, car loans, and credit cards.

Priority 3: Fully fund your money shield to 3+ months to cover the 4 walls plus insurance.
- Plan for large purchases by saving for them just like any other budget item, such as a 20% down payment on a home, elective medical procedures, and education.

Priority 4: Focus on increasing your investment percentage contributions:

- Aim for 5% of your income in year 1.
- Aim for 10% of your income in year 2.
- Aim for 15% to 20% of your income in year 3 and beyond.

Priority 5: Develop a long-term mentality to continue increasing your human capital.
- Find a mentor.
- Hire a financial advisor.
- Continue learning.

If you don't have debt:

Priority 1: Fully fund your money shield to 3+ months to cover the 4 walls plus insurance.
- Plan for large purchases by saving for them just like any other budget item, such as a 20% down payment for a home, elective medical procedures, and additional education.

Priority 2: Focus on increasing your investment percentage contributions:
- Aim for 5% of your income in year 1.
- Aim for 10% of your income in year 2.
- Aim for 15% to 20% of your income in year 3 and

beyond.

Priority 3: Develop a long-term mentality to continue increasing your human capital.
- Find a mentor.
- Hire a financial advisor.
- Continue learning.

To make the case that a person should first use money as a means of protection, let's look at Maslow's hierarchy of needs. In 1943, American psychologist Abraham Maslow developed a theory representing human needs in a hierarchical pyramid format where the needs at the bottom of the pyramid needed to be satisfied first before the ones on top could be achieved. From bottom to top, the five needs he outlined were: physiological needs, safety needs, belongingness and love needs, esteem needs, and self-actualization needs. The bottom two categories are often called a person's basic needs. Physiological needs speak to our most basic requirements such as access to food and water, keeping our bodies warm, and being able to rest. Safety needs relate to our need to feel safe in our environment. In financial terms, basic needs translate to the need of protecting the 4 financial walls (food, access to basic home utilities like electricity and water, a roof over your head, and access to transportation). When these needs are met, one can expand and achieve higher levels of financial safety. This latter piece can be achieved with proper insurance coverage, such as health and life insurance.

Having a money shield to protect you against bad luck is a giant step toward financial security. As a rule of thumb, it is recommended you have at least 3 to 6 months of your monthly expenses saved up to cover unfortunate life events. The money shield provides a buffer against things that can go wrong in life such as job loss, injury, or an unexpected expense like a car repair. Some people, including myself, strive to have as much as 12 months of coverage. Why 3 or 6 or 12 months? In my situation, it is based on how long it would take me to find a similar job in the event I lose my current one. The recruiting process for my type of job can take several months. Another way to think about it is by estimating, if you were injured or sick, how long would you need to recover and then find a new job, assuming you were let go from your previous one.

The peace of mind I've gained from having a money shield allows me to think long-term and not be bothered about the short-term ups and downs that happen in life. I make better decisions and live better than I would otherwise.

What should you include as your monthly expenses for the

emergency fund? Leverage Maslow's basic needs as guidance, and include the expenses associated with taking care of the 4 walls (rent/mortgage, utilities, food, transportation). Also, include the level 2 type of safety needs as well. This means items such as insurance premiums and a will. If something happens to your income, you want to have enough saved to continue to cover your health and life insurance, for example.

If you are a young adult and in good health with no spouse and no dependents, insurance may sound like a waste of your money. However, sooner or later you will grow your assets and realize you are not immune to bad things that happen in life. Insurance is there to protect you and to protect your valuables against risk. You have so many risks to consider: someone stealing your identity and opening up credit cards in your name, getting in a car accident, your house catching fire, illness, the inability to work for a long period, death. Enough, right?

Let's look at the different types of insurance coverage you should have or at least know about for the future.

Auto insurance: Car insurance is a requirement if you have a vehicle in your name. The decision you need to make here is concerning what level of coverage do you need. How much coverage do you need to protect yourself versus protecting the other parties' property and lives in the event of an accident? It is prudent for you to shop around and discuss your current situation with an insurance agent to determine the appropriate level of coverage you are comfortable with. Ask a licensed agent about the following common types of coverages: liability (covers injuries, damages, and death you cause), bodily injury (this covers funeral and medical expenses of people involved in the accident, except for you), collision (covers damages to your vehicle), comprehensive (covers damages not related to an accident like vandalism or falling objects), uninsured driver (covers if you are a victim of a hit-and-run situation or when someone doesn't have insurance), and no-fault (state-specific, requires all drivers to insure themselves). You can call individual insurance companies or contact a broker who will shop and compare multiple carriers so you can price shop more easily. Ask if the carriers provide discounts based on who your employer is, the college you graduated from, the type of job you have, or if you already have another policy with them. This is an exercise you should do every year your policy renews to make sure you are always getting the best deal.

Home/renters insurance: If you own a home and have a mortgage, then you already have insurance on the property since the lender requires it. Home insurance pays if there are damages to the property or injuries to someone who is visiting your property. You should review this policy yearly by getting a quote from a broker who can shop multiple carriers. Ask them for discounts based on your employer, college, organizations you belong to, and type of job you have. Make sure you go over with the agent all the different types of coverage and amounts you have. Discuss any expensive possessions you have in the house to see if they are covered (e.g. jewelry, instruments, artwork). Also check for savings if you have security features in your home like alarms or a sprinkler system. If you rent, check out renters insurance to protect your belongings even though you don't own the property. Policies can be very affordable and are especially important if you have expensive belongings.

Health insurance: Auto and home insurance will typically not cover you if you end up needing medical help. That's what health insurance is for. There are at least two major categories to know in your health insurance: hospitalization and medical coverage. Hospitalization coverage covers expenses like the cost of your hospital room, lab tests, medications, and nurse care. Medical insurance covers doctor bills related to your hospital visit. Given the astronomical cost of health care in the U.S., health insurance is extremely important to have. People go bankrupt due to medical debt. Learn what type of coverage is available to you from either your parents, school, employer, or the government. If none of these options are available, you can buy your own. The important questions you need to be able to answer for your financial planning are: What is your premium? What is your deductible? And, what is your maximum out-of-pocket expense? Knowing these answers allows you to estimate how much financial coverage you need. (do the same for vision and dental insurance if applicable to you). There are several different types of plans to learn about such as PPOs (preferred provider organizations), HMOs (health maintenance organizations), and HSAs (health savings accounts). Health Savings Accounts are designed to have lower premiums but require a higher deductible. They have a very interesting feature that allows you to save and invest the money tax-deferred and use the funds tax-free if used to pay for qualified health expenses. We will discuss HSAs further in Move #4.

Life insurance: Life insurance is first and foremost a protective product even though it is often pitched as an investment product as well. The death benefit is distributed to the beneficiaries of the policy income tax-free and without passing through probate. The argument for having life insurance becomes very strong when you have anyone who would suffer financial loss if you were to die today. This could be a spouse, child, parent, or anyone else who you care about and depends on you. Even if you are young without many possessions, you could still get a small amount of coverage for funeral expenses. Funeral expenses continue to trend up, averaging somewhere around $7,000 to $12,000. Take a minute and ask yourself, "If I were to die today who would incur a financial loss and how much would they need?" If you can think of someone, then consider getting life insurance. Many employers offer a group life policy; however, that expires the moment you leave that job.

Two types of insurance coverage you can consider purchasing are term and permanent.

Term insurance policies provide coverage for a specific period of time. There is no death benefit after the policy expires. It is the most affordable type of life insurance and it is often known as pure insurance.

Permanent insurance, also known as cash value policies, offers coverage for your entire life without an expiration date. They not only offer a protection feature (death benefit), they allow you to accumulate cash as either savings or investments (depending on the type of policy you purchase).

Make sure to ask and understand the following questions when you speak with an agent: How much coverage do I need for my situation and why? What term do you suggest and why? Will my premium ever change? How much of my premium goes toward the insurance part vs. fees vs. investments? Can I access the cash value and at what cost? Will the policy ever expire? Is the carrier in good financial condition? Make sure you only terminate an insurance policy after you've confirmed you have coverage with another company. This way you won't go without coverage. And, feel free to call a different agent if you don't like the answers you get.

Identity theft restoration: When ID theft happens to you, you will need help restoring your identity and clearing your name. Cyber-criminals may steal not only your credit cards, but also perhaps your social security number, medical records, open loans on your name, your unemployment check, and much more. The key aspect you need to look for when signing up for ID theft coverage is to make sure you sign up for a program that will not only monitor for identity theft, but will also help you resolve your issue by assigning a team to spend the numerous hours on the phone needed and to do the paperwork required to fix the problem. Another aspect to look for is coverage of legal expenses, loss of income, and potential out-of-pocket costs you may incur due to the loss. Check first with your home or renters' insurance to see if you already have this benefit with the other policy before you purchase ID theft restoration.

Long-term disability insurance: In the event you have an accident or an illness that disables you from doing your job for an extended amount of time, long-term disability insurance can replace a percentage of your income and help you cover your living expenses for some time (often for two years, five years, or to age 65). This insurance option is often offered through your employer. However, you can also purchase this coverage on your own. Make sure you understand and agree on the definition of disability if you are purchasing on your own. Furthermore, states often require employers to hold workers' compensation benefits to cover employees that are injured on the job as an alternative to litigation. Other benefits could be available from your state, or perhaps through social security. The task here is for you to educate yourself and inquire with your employer's human resources team to learn what options are available. If you are unsatisfied with what you learn, reach out to an insurance broker or carrier to see if you can find appropriate coverage.

Long-term care insurance: Particularly if you are 60 or older, consider getting long-term care insurance. If you are far from this age, tell your parents or grandparents about this. Long-term care insurance will pay for the very expensive services one may need from nursing homes, in-home care professionals, and assisted living facilities. Considering our population is living longer and the cost of care can add up to thousands of dollars per month, it is prudent to investigate having coverage while you are healthy. Don't assume that Medicare or Medicaid will cover all the costs you may need for long-term care. Reach out to an agent who can discuss your specific situation. Also, make sure to check your health insurance and life insurance policies to see if they offer any benefit for these situations.

Last but not least, do you have a will in place? This isn't a monthly expense per se, but it is a component of your safety needs. A will is the first step and most basic document for estate planning. It is not only for the wealthy and old. A will is a legally binding document in which you spell out exactly what you wish to happen to your possessions after you die. This is important to everyone, but it is especially important if you have a spouse or a partner and any children. The will can outline who will serve as guardians to your minor children. Understand that if you die without a will, the state you live in will step in and make decisions on what to do with your possessions and who should be guardians for your children. This process is called probate, and it can be costly and long. Essentially, your loved ones will need to go through the legal system to resolve any matters associated with your estate. Unless you don't mind the government making decisions on your behalf after you die, I highly suggest you get a will. Please do not procrastinate.

Now that we've become more educated on what needs to be captured in your money shield (enough to cover the 4 walls plus insurance), where should you save the money?

My suggestion is to open a separate account dedicated only to the emergency fund. Use your current bank and search for a savings account that doesn't have any fees or minimums and is FDIC insured. Many online savings accounts may offer a higher yield on your money and no fees or minimums, which are good options for those starting as well. If you'd like to explore other options, consider a money market account that may offer higher earnings than some checking or savings accounts while still being very liquid. You could also open a CD to earn more interest, though, the money may not be as easily accessible as the other options without a penalty. Although it's okay to chase higher yields for your rainy-day fund, remember that the main purpose of it is to have immediate access to it in case of an emergency. The end of this chapter has a link with resources of where you can open your account.

A quick note if you have debt: focus on creating a smaller version of your emergency fund first. Rather than focusing on 3+ months of coverage, aim for 1 month of coverage. Once you are out debt, then refocus on fully funding it to 3+

months. For everyone else, multiply the average of your monthly expenses by three (or more) to get the amount you need in savings to cover you for three months (or more) of expenses. That amount will be your savings goal. This money is designed to secure a roof over your head, put food on the table, provide water to shower, and give you a means of transportation for 3 whole months or more.

MOVE 2: GET YOUR PRIORITIES RIGHT

Key Action Items
Visit **rebrand.ly/MoneyMoves**
for more resources.

1. Know how you will prioritize the use of your money – money shield, debt reduction, and investments.
2. Learn about the most common insurance types and list them on a piece of paper. Ask and answer: do I already have it? Do I need it? Can I get a quote to compare and price shop? Include this cost as part of your money shield. Visit the website above for more resources.
3. Get a will in place. Visit the website above for more

resources.

4. Determine the target size of your money shield: 1x if you are in debt, +3x if you are out of debt. Add up your monthly expenses and multiply the total by 1, 3, or more. This will determine the amount you need.

Open a separate account dedicated to the money shield. Visit the website above for more resources.

STOP MAKING THE BANKS RICH. BE INTENTIONAL WITH YOUR MONEY

MOVE 3:
SHRINK TODAY & EXPAND YOUR TOMORROW

> "The quickest way to double your money is to fold it in half and put it in your back pocket."
>
> Will Rogers

We often waste a lot of time and money doing and buying things that don't align with where we are financially. Do you ever catch yourself comparing your lifestyle to someone else's? Perhaps you see your friends or relatives going on fancy vacations and wish you could do the same? Do you get so emotional about it that you go out and charge your credit card with items you can't afford?

It's time to stop comparing and stop digging that hole.

You will likely never achieve financial security if you can't control your spending behavior. Debt can be a massive problem in a person's life. It can rob your peace of mind and financial freedom. It can cloud your judgment and create massive levels of stress. It can also result in having your possessions taken away from you or worse, like going to jail if you owe taxes. Eliminate debt as soon as possible. The only debt you can exclude from your immediate list of items to pay extra is your mortgage if you own a home. Yes, you should still pay your mortgage and work toward paying off your home. However, the nature of real estate debt is a bit different as it is a real asset that tends to go up in value over time. Take a moment to assess the level of debt you're in today. Leverage the financial dashboard to get insights. Is your net worth positive or negative? Is your net income over the past couple of months positive or negative?

Be confident that you can have any lifestyle you desire. However, if you're in a situation where you are mostly in the red, you should approach the problem both from an income perspective and from a spending perspective. Focus on shrinking your lifestyle as much as possible. Additionally, focus on finding ways to make more money by working more hours or taking side jobs to boost your income. These actions combined will help you get out of debt faster. Remember that this is temporary pain until you get back on track. Apply the savings you generate to build up your 1-month money shield first, then pay off the debt as fast as you can. Pay off the debts with higher interest first while making the minimum payments for the others. Leverage the debt list you created in Move #1 to keep track and update the balance as you pay things off. Print it or write it down on a piece of paper and have it visible in your house. Review it monthly at a minimum.

Now, let's get more tactical and focused on how to reduce your monthly expenses.

First, organize your monthly expenses from highest to lowest and ask the following question for each expense category: *is this a want or is this a need?* You can accomplish this by looking at them on the online platform you've signed up for or by writing them down on a piece of paper (or using a spreadsheet). List them on the left side of the screen or paper and fill in your answers to the above question with the word *want* or *need* next to each category. Make sure you answer the questions honestly.

Second, eliminate the items you've classified as *wants* instead of *needs*. How do you eliminate them? Simply stop buying them or doing them until you are no longer broke.

Third, leverage the online money management tool to set goals (like funding your money shield), plan your monthly budget, and track your daily spending. A budget is simply a plan of how you will direct and use your money over a time period. I suggest you budget at least monthly. Plan next month's budget a few days before the end of the month. Start by estimating how much money you will make, then list all your expenses and decide how much you will spend on them. Think ahead for holidays and birthdays expenses. When setting these spending goals, they should be specific, measurable, attainable, relevant, and time-based (S.M.A.R.T). As discussed, eliminate your *wants* and trim down your *needs* if possible. Fixed items like rent should be easier to plan and estimate, while variable items like food and restaurants or entertainment require you to be intentional about setting a lower amount for the month. The online budget tools will do a nice job helping you set the target amounts by category and track your spending as you go, assuming you pay with cards. If there is a category you don't pay with a card, set the budgeted cash amount in an envelope, and withdraw the money as you go. When the money is gone, then you've hit your budget for the period. If for some reason you are not using the online platforms, create your budget in a spreadsheet or notebook. The end goal is to apply the savings or the extra income you make toward the debt. See more at the end of this chapter for ideas to make more money in the short-term.

A side note for when you feel overwhelmed dealing with

your finances: you don't need to always be perfect. It is most important that you are intentional and have a continuous improvement mindset.

A technique you can use to identify what to focus on and prioritize is the 80/20 rule. The 80/20 rule, also known as the Pareto Principle, states that about 80% of the effects come from about 20% of the causes. Vilfredo Pareto was an Italian economist who noticed that 80% of the peas in his garden came from about 20% of the pea pods. He then observed similar behavior in other areas. For example, around 20% of the landowners in Italy owned about 80% of the land. This behavior has been well observed across many areas of life, including in business and investments.

This concept can be used as a tool to identify the less important many from the most important few. Sort your monthly expenses in a descending table format where your highest cost categories are displayed on top and the lower cost categories are at the bottom. Next, divide each category by the total spending so you get the percentage contribution to the total of each category. You will likely notice that if you add the percentage share of the first few expense items, you will end up with a large percentage of the total for the category. This helps you identify what expense items have the biggest influence in your monthly budget or expense category. For example, say you are looking at your monthly eating out expenses and you identify 5 main restaurants where you spent a total of $150. The breakdown of how you spent your money was sushi $50, Italian $30, Thai $25, burgers $25, tacos $20. If you apply the 80/20 rule, you discover that 70% of your eating out budget is spent on the first three categories. And, most of the money is spent on your monthly sushi adventure (33%). Because you are trying to save money and budget better, you decide to skip sushi from now on and put $600 back in your pocket (if you do this for a year). You've just identified and prioritized the item that moved the scale the most in this example.

So, how will you know if you are doing better financially? Your financial dashboard with the 3 KFIs – net worth, net income, and credit score – provides you with that information. Your net worth should be increasing over time, your net income should be consistently positive over time, and your credit score should be trending up as you deal with debt better. Monitor these key financial indicators at least monthly. Remember to keep the pressure on your lifestyle and expenses until all debts are paid (except your mortgage if you have one; pay it regularly). When the debt is gone, finish building up your money shield to at least 3 months. Finally, with a fully loaded emergency fund, you can start being more aggressive toward investments. If your employer gives you a match on your retirement account, consider pushing pause on contributions if your plan to be out of debt is within 24 months. If that's not for you, contribute the maximum amount the employer will match. We will discuss investments in more detail in the next chapter.

One more important note before you continue: if you believe your spending behavior is completely out of control and you know that you have very little self-control, please consider having an honest conversation with a health care professional about your behavior. Some people may have a biochemical imbalance or perhaps trauma that hinders their self-control. This situation needs to be addressed as it becomes nearly impossible to win with money if you can't control yourself.

For inspiration, let me give you a personal example of how I handled my debt.

I was $33,000 in debt when I finished graduate school in Pennsylvania, and I wanted to pay it off as soon as possible. Upon graduation, I was extended a well-paying job that required I moved to Oregon for at least one year. I did not own a car at the time and had about $800 in my bank account. So, I took the job and went to work, not only at my job, but on my finances.

Instead of going to a car dealership waving my job offer to ask for a car loan, I landed in Portland and took the MAX light-rail train line straight to a thrift store and bought a used bicycle. I found a cheap apartment to rent near my employer so I could walk or bike to work. I furnished my apartment with basic household items from either a thrift store or garage sales. I even bought some black trash bags to use as curtains for my bedroom. I understand this wasn't pretty, but I was $33,000 in debt. I also knew that my pain was temporary. If I could limit my spending, I'd be out of debt in around 12 months. Then I'd be able to start thinking about the future. I spent the first few weeks saving all the money I possibly could until I had an emergency fund to cover my basic needs for about 1 month. That gave me some breathing room psychologically. I then threw everything I could on the debt and hit my goal of paying it off in as soon as possible. After my debt was paid and my emergency fund was fully funded, I began funding my retirement and other investments. My employer at the time didn't provide a 401(k) match, so I didn't contribute during the first year. Why am I telling you this story? Because I hope it will motivate you to improve your financial condition. The pain is temporary, and paying off that debt is the greatest feeling in the world.

If you are not in debt and budgeting consistently, make sure you've built up your money shield to at least 3 months of coverage and contribute to your retirement account (more on Move #4). You can still review your lifestyle and find ways to be more cost-efficient.

How much more?

Well, how about I challenge you to reduce your spending by 10% for at least 12 months? If you can maintain this level of savings for at least 1 year, that would be the equivalent of adding more than 1 month of coverage to your emergency fund or additional money that you can apply toward investments. Perhaps this slight reduction in your expenses would free up room for you to boost your retirement contributions and get you faster to retirement. On the other hand, if lifestyle reduction is not for you right now, how about you try to make 10% more money? Consider a short-term sprint where for a few months you work extra hours or take a side job for a little while and apply the extra funds toward speeding up your retirement. That could lead to massive benefits in the long term.

The message here is that you can always do a little better. Leverage the online money management platform to set goals, budget, and track your progress. Otherwise, you can do the same in a spreadsheet or using a pencil and paper.

Let's take a deeper look into some practical ideas on how to save and make more money in the short term, regardless if you are in debt or not.

Ideas to Save Money

MONEY MOVES

1. Get rid of stuff. Examples would include: cutting cable TV and online streaming and visiting the library instead; drinking coffee at home instead of at a coffee shop; eating at home instead of in a restaurant; taking a break from bars and enjoying more time at home or at a friend's house; waiting 24 hours before making a purchase; buying used instead of new; and selling your expensive car and getting a cheaper one.
    o Cars are money pits. They will keep you broke as they rapidly depreciate and are expensive to run and maintain. Buy a low-cost used vehicle that has already substantially depreciated. You need it for transportation, not to show off to your friends.

2. Negotiate it down. Examples would include: calling your credit card company and asking for a lower interest rate or transferring your balance to a card with lower interest; calling your internet provider and asking for a discount; and asking for a reduction in your medical bill amount. If you don't ask for something, you will likely never get it.

3. Get a roommate to split rent with you or consider moving somewhere cheaper. This could be one of your biggest money-saving events. As a rule of thumb, aim to keep your rent or mortgage below 25% of your take

home income. Still too hard? Get more roommates or make more money.

4. Consolidate your debts with a debt consolidation loan to reduce your overall interest rate. Just watch for excessive fees.

5. Shop with coupons. Search for couponing Apps and have them easily available on your smartphone.

Ideas to Make Money

1. Ask for more hours at your current job. Let your employer know you are on a journey to improve your financial life and you're looking for more opportunities to earn more.

2. Sell something you haven't used in 12 months. Look around your house and look for items you could easily sell online.

3. Start side jobs to boost your income. Examples include pizza delivery, driving for a rideshare company like Uber or Lyft, and getting paid to grocery shop for companies like Instacart or Shipt.

4. Look for freelance opportunities on websites like Upwork or Toptal.

5. Offer your services in your neighborhood to mow grass, walk dogs, babysit, pet sit, or housesit.

A quick note if you are dealing with debt collectors: Debt collectors are paid to recover unpaid debt, and many of them will use nasty tactics to make you feel guilty or threatened so you pay them immediately. If you owe, you should pay. However, you can negotiate a lower payment. If you do, get it in writing. Also, know that debt collectors need to respect federal law (search for the Fair Debt Collection Practices Act); they can't harass you in the middle of the night, for example. If possible, record and document all your conversations. Also, never give them access to your bank account. Pay them with a money order or cashier's check.

MOVE 3: SHRINK TODAY AND EXPAND YOUR TOMORROW

Key Action Items
Visit **rebrand.ly/MoneyMoves**
for more resources.

1. Determine your situation based on net worth and net income. Are you positive or negative?

2. Sort your monthly expenses top to bottom, then ask and answer, "Is it a need or want?" Eliminate the wants and reduce the needs.

3. If your situation is negative, get fired up about reducing your lifestyle and boosting your income. Apply the savings to get a 1-month money shield fund in place, then pay off your debts. Use the online tools to set budgets and keep track of your progress. Consider pausing retirement

contributions if you eliminate your debt in less than 24 months. Next, fully fund the emergency fund to 3x or more. Then, resume retirement savings.

If your situation is positive, fully fund your money shield and contribute to retirement. Optional: reduce your expenses by 10% and improve your income by an additional 10% for a period of time. Apply the savings to retirement or other investments.

MOVE 4:
INVEST NOW FOR YOUR FUTURE

> "Compound interest is the eighth wonder of the world. He who understands it, earns it... he who doesn't... pays it."
>
> Albert Einstein

How different will your mindset be when you have your debts paid off and a fully-funded money shield? I noticed my shoulders felt lighter during the day and I slept better at night once I arrived at this milestone. For some reason, I also found myself to be slightly more courageous to speak my mind at work, as opposed to being a "yes" type of person. I no longer felt I was fighting a fire whenever I got a bill I wasn't expecting. In short, I began making better decisions in my life since I had a buffer between me and random bad events. A basic level of financial security empowered me to dedicate my efforts toward the next step in the journey to financial freedom: investing.

Investments and debt are opposites. Debt gives you something today by taking from your future, whereas an investment is the exchange of something from today (cash, for example) into an asset you hope will grow and generate more value in the future (such as a stock). Investments require time to grow and are exposed to risks. The asset may go up or down in value over time, and you do run the risk of losing it all. However, more often than not, the overall long-term trend is that you will end up with more money than what you started with if you can hold steady during challenging times. Hence, another reason I strongly recommend having a money shield is to enable you to not panic and sell your investments during trying times. To earn higher returns, one is typically exposed to higher risks, while a lower risk investment often translates to lower returns. Therefore, if you want your money to grow to a sizable amount in the future, you will likely need to get comfortable with some level of risk exposure.

As an example, the S&P 500 index, a benchmark of the American stock market performance, has enjoyed a nominal average return of around 10% since its inception in 1926. However, the index experiences a lot of volatility. In 2008, the index returned -37.2% while in 2009 and 2010 it returned a positive +27.11% and +14.87%, respectively. Investing requires a steady hand, and a person needs to be ready emotionally and financially to ride the ups and downs. Many financial institutions offer tools for you to learn more about your appetite for risk and suggestions on how to allocate your investments given your age and goals. You may find yourself to be more conservative or more aggressive. Knowing your risk appetite profile enables you to have perspective on what types of investments are best suited to you. Visit the web link at the bottom of this chapter to gain access to online tools to help you learn more about your risk appetite profile before you start investing.

Considering there is a risk when investing, why should you invest at all? Because investing allows you to make money outside of your regular job. Investments can grow to very large sums that may provide you with more money than what you could make alone working a job. It took me a few years but eventually, I experienced this situation in my own retirement accounts. At first, the returns seemed to be small. However, there was a tipping point around June 2016 when the returns on my retirement accounts exceeded the amount of money I could save in a month. This was only about 3 years after I paid off my student debt. In other words, investments can provide you with true financial freedom.

Although retirement may seem like it is a long way away, it's really not. And you don't want to realize that when you're older and have far less money than you could have had if you had invested at a much younger age.

A very important concept to understand now is compounding. As an example, if you start investing $100 at the beginning of each month at age 25 with an average 10% annual return on your money, you will have $637,676 at age 65. However, if you wait 10 years to start on this journey, you would have just $227,932 at age 65. That's a $409,744 gap because you waited 10 years to start investing. That is the power of compounding returns over a long period of time.

Time in the market is fundamental to build up sizable assets. If you are thinking, "I'm in debt, but I shouldn't pay anything off. I should invest first." Wrong! Why? Three reasons:

- The interest rate you may be paying on your debts may be impossible to achieve with regular investment returns.
- If something goes wrong in your life, you can pause your investments but not your debts.
- You are likely to be more emotionally unstable,

leading you to make hasty financial decisions.

So how do you start learning about investments? First, let's get familiar with a few different vehicles you can use to make investments.

Typically, you have options to invest with pre-tax or post-tax dollars. Investing pre-tax means that you are funding the account with money that has not yet been taxed by the government; you are saving on paying taxes now. You may, however, be taxed when you withdraw the money in the future. This will depend if the account is treated as tax-deferred (pay later) or tax-free (no tax liability). Investing post-tax means you are funding the account with money you've already paid taxes on. You may, however, still need to pay taxes on the growth or the gains in the future. Let's review some common investment accounts.

Common retirement accounts like a 401(k) and 403(b) are employer-sponsored plans in which you can make contributions to your retirement with either pre-tax or post-tax dollars. Post-tax accounts would be called Roth 401(k) or Roth 403(b). It's important to know that many employers offer what is known as a matching contribution to your retirement account.

As an example, if you contribute $100 into your retirement account, your employer may match your contribution with another $100. This is free money toward your retirement and an immediate 100% gain on your investment. Ask your human resources department to find out if your employer offers any kind of matching contribution. If so, make it a goal to invest at least the minimum amount you need to take maximum advantage of the employer matching contribution. Ideally, if you do the math of your contribution plus the employer's match, you'd want to see around 5% of your income being saved for retirement as a starting point. If there is no match, you should still aim to start by saving at least 5% of your income. Why do I suggest 5%? Because it is way better than 0%, it's a solid starting point, and it is easier to process psychologically since you won't be seeing that money anytime soon. As you gain control of your financial life, you will want to bump this percentage closer to 15% to 20%, or the maximum contribution allowed by the IRS.

When you get to this point, I expect you to be more financially savvy than you are right now, especially if you follow my recommendation in Move #5, and you will be able to make decisions on your own. Going back to what to ask HR, inquire if there is a vesting period. A vesting period is an amount of time you need to be employed by the company before the employer matching contributions become fully yours.

The next step will be to determine where to invest the money you are investing.

There are different types of assets you can invest in, each with a different level of risk and return profile. Common types include stocks and bonds.

When you purchase a stock, also known as equity, you are buying a small piece of a business that is traded on a stock exchange. As part owner of the business, you participate in the gains of the company when the business does well and becomes more valuable (known as capital gains). You may also receive additional stock or a cash distribution as the business distributes its earnings over time (known as a dividend payment). Remember that businesses don't always go up in value or pay dividends.

Bonds, on the other hand, are essentially what is known as an I.O.U. An investor lends money to a commercial or government institution, and in return he or she is promised a return of the amount lent (principal) plus interest over an agreed period of time. Bonds are typically seen as less risky than stocks.

As a small investor, it is typically not recommended you spend time trying to pick individual stocks or bonds for your retirement considering that the risk of loss is very high. To overcome this issue, investors diversify their investment into many stocks, bonds, and other asset classes like commodities or real estate. This diversification into many assets creates a portfolio in which the risk is spread across winners and losers. Therefore, the investor is not dependent on the success of only one or two companies.

For example, imagine you have $10,000 to invest for retirement. Instead of picking one stock to invest all your money, you decide to spread your investment across hundreds of stocks. That means your portfolio returns will be dependent on a large pool of investments, and in the event a company goes under, you won't lose all your investment. Vehicles you can use to accomplish this type of diversification are mutual funds and/or exchange-traded funds that either actively invest in or track the performance of hundreds of companies.

A mutual fund is actively managed, meaning there is a group of professionals actively trading assets trying to achieve higher returns.

Exchange-traded funds are not actively managed. Instead, they try to mimic the performance and behavior of an index. The most common indexes the market follows are the Dow Jones Industrial Average and the S&P 500 Index. These indices track the performance of a list of representative companies treated as a proxy for the broad economy.

It is prudent you have a conversation with a licensed professional to get more educated on these matters. Ask your employer to connect you with a licensed professional of the financial institution your retirement account is in. This professional can typically discuss investment options factoring in your age and risk appetite profile, often at no direct cost to you. I also recommend you ask the financial professional what fees are being charged on your investments. Fees can eat up your returns over time, so discuss finding low-cost options.

Next up are Individual Retirement Accounts, also known as IRAs. These are self-managed accounts you can leverage in addition to your employer-sponsored plans or if you don't have access to an employer-sponsored plan. Contributions can be tax-deductible for traditional plans and after-tax for what is known as a Roth IRA. The money in the traditional IRA grows tax-deferred (pay the tax later) while the Roth IRA grows tax-free (you've paid already). IRAs offer great flexibility from an investment choice perspective. This is different than the employer-sponsored retirement accounts in which investment options may be more limited. Once again, I recommend speaking with a licensed professional before deciding where to invest your retirement money. Be aware that the Internal Revenue Service (IRS) has set rules and income limits for IRAs.

A final word on retirement accounts is that they are typically protected against creditors. This is a further incentive to contribute to these accounts over your working years.

Let's now revisit a little bit of our conversation on how much should you invest in retirement.

I mentioned 5% of your income is a good start whether you get an employer match or not. I also said that you will eventually want to bump up your contributions to 15% or 20%, or perhaps the maximum allowed amount by the IRS. However, remember that at the end of the day, it will all depend on how wealthy you want to be and how fast do you want to get there. Everyone has different goals and circumstances that need to be considered. Therefore, I highly recommend you talk to a licensed financial professional who can discuss your situation with you.

Another important question you want to answer is: "How much should I strive to have in retirement?" For educational purposes, I'll share that a rule of thumb is to have around 70% of your current income during retirement. That means that if today you make $50,000 per year, you should target to have around $35,000 coming in per year in retirement. Where would this money come from? Largely from the investments you made throughout your working years.

Let's look at the math:

I'm going to ignore Social Security for this conversation since we don't know what will happen to the program decades from now. If you do end up getting Social Security checks when you retire, then that's gravy on the top for you.

So, what amount do you need to have to be able to withdraw $35,000 per year? A good initial target would be about $875,000. This is based on a rule of thumb developed from academic research stating that a person should be able to withdraw 4% of their portfolio value per year with little risk of running out of money. So, divide your desired retirement income amount per year by 0.04, and that will give you a target for the total sum of money you'd need in your portfolio at retirement. In our example we divide $35,000 by 4% to get $875,000 dollars. This rule of thumb is not infallible, but it does provide you with a good ballpark target to strive for.

Now that you have a target, it is up to you to determine how fast you want to get there. Do you remember our compounding example of investing only $100 per month and how it grows to a large sum over time? You must start investing soon so you have time on your side.

Here is a quick review of steps you can take over time:

- Keep it simple and save whatever you can at first (be out of debt).
- Contribute at least 5% with or without a match.
- Try to increase your contributions by 5% the next year and every year after that until you get to 15%-20% of your income. If you can do more,

contribute to the maximum allowed amount by law per year.

- If you get fired up, invest outside of retirement accounts to build your portfolio even faster.
- Remember to leverage the online budgeting tools to keep track of your progress to see how your net worth is growing over time.
- As you progress in your career and earn salary increases or promotions, maintain your lifestyle and divert those new funds to your retirement accounts.

Retirement is a large topic and a goal for many of us. However, so is the desire to buy a home or to make another large purchase. Think ahead and plan to save for these expected purchases such as a car, wedding ring, wedding, nice vacation, or perhaps a medical procedure you will need. Treat them like planned budget items and leverage the online platforms to help you plan and save so you don't borrow more money.

For those who wish to buy a home, I suggest that you try to save for at least a 20% down payment and keep your payment below 25% of your monthly income. This would result in more favorable terms with your lender. And if you've been good about handling your debts and if you kept track of the third KFI (your credit score), you may enjoy lower interest rates when asking for a home loan. When the time comes, evaluate the payment terms for a 15-year fixed interest term or a 30-year fixed interest term. If you can handle the 15-year term, you would save a significant amount in interest payments over the years. However, there are other factors you need to consider, such as how long you plan to live in the home, if you will have paying roommates, and if you prefer to save and invest the difference in the payment terms between the 30-year or the 15-year loans. A financial professional would be able to help you understand these tradeoffs.

After you have fully funded your emergency fund, consider setting up a separate account where you can save monthly for your down payment, if that's a goal you have. Remember that not everyone needs to buy a home, especially if you think you will be moving frequently or if you think that your situation will change in the near future (examples would include getting married and having children).

It is mostly okay for you to temporarily pause or reduce some of your retirement funding to save for a down payment for a home. A home is very important and is part of your basic financial needs. Whether you decide to pay off your home with cash or in 15 or 30 years, try to pay it off by retirement.

As a side note, if you are more passionate about investing in real estate than in retirement accounts, that is also a good approach, in my opinion. Just be sure to manage your exposure to debt and have enough saved in your emergency fund.

Let's now broaden our conversation to other investment accounts you can leverage as you become more mature and savvier, including brokerage accounts, 529s and ESAs for education purposes, and HSAs for health care expenses.

Cash Brokerage Account: This is a taxable account into which you deposit cash with a licensed brokerage firm. This account allows you to trade a variety of financial assets, including stocks and bonds. The brokerage firm will execute on your trades and may charge a commission fee. There is no limit on how much you can add to the account. Be careful, though: a tax liability may exist on capital gains or income you may receive from the assets. If you are just starting out, leave this type of account for a little later when you have your debt under control and an emergency fund in place. This is not considered a retirement account.

529s & ESAs: Many parents think ahead and plan for their kids' college education. There are two main options to pick from that offer tax-free benefits when used for college expenses: either a 529 plan or a Coverdell Education Savings Account. Here are some of the consideration points for each:

- 529 has no age limit for using the funds while the ESA has to be used by 30.
- The contribution limit per year for the 529 is much larger than the ESA.
- 529 has less flexibility on your ability to pick where the money will be invested in.
- The 529 plan is for college only while ESA can be used for primary or secondary education.
- The ESA has income restrictions.

HSAs: The health savings account, also known as Medical IRA, is an option available for those who are enrolled in a high-deductible health plan. The HSA offers you a triple tax advantage by allowing you to save the money pre-tax (reducing your tax liability today), invest the money tax-free, and use the money for qualified medical expenses tax-free. Unfortunately, in the event you need to use the money for non-qualified expenses, the IRS will penalize you with fees and taxes. Considering the rise in health care costs, an HSA can be a good option, especially if you can leave the money invested for many years so that compound returns can do their magic and grow your overall balance. However, that would require you to be able to cover your current medical expenses with the money you have available today.

I've discussed a great deal in this chapter. As you've seen, there are many ways to invest for your future. Many people miss out on opportunities because they are not aware of the possibilities. It is up to you to search and learn more about these and many more other topics. Review the action items below, take proper action, and proceed to the next chapter where we will discuss the importance of having a long-term growth mindset and ideas you can entertain for your future.

MOVE 4: INVEST NOW FOR YOUR FUTURE

Key Action Items
Visit **rebrand.ly/MoneyMoves**
for more resources.

1. Determine your investor risk profile and gain insights on sample asset allocations for your personality.

2. Reach out to your employer and inquire about any retirement matching and vesting period. Target 5% of your income toward retirement, then increase the contribution by 5% every year until you reach 15-20% or the max IRS amount. If fired up, save more in other accounts as allowed by law.

3. Speak with a financial professional to help you determine how to invest the money given your investor profile, and inquire about using low-cost investments to save on fees.

4. Discuss with an advisor or use the 4% rule to estimate how much you need to replace your income in retirement.

5. Treat large purchases as planned budget items with the online tools at your disposal. Aim for at least 20% when buying a home.

6. Familiarize yourself with cash brokerage accounts, education accounts, and health savings accounts. Determine if you need or are ready for them.

MONEY MOVES

THINK AHEAD AND GET AHEAD

MOVE 5:
HAVE A LONG-TERM GROWTH ACTION PLAN

"Growth inside fuels growth outside."

John C. Maxwell

People often share with me how they seldom think about their future. There are so many options and so many paths in life, it is easy to rationalize that you have zero control of what will happen to you in the future. Their life philosophy is purely carpe diem, or "seize the day." Well, I'd like to challenge you that although carpe diem has its place, one should periodically stop and take stock of where they are in life. Are you productive or are you partying 24/7? You should then evaluate your direction and determine if you should keep doing what you're doing or change paths. What are some possible future outcomes for those who are productive and continue with this behavior over time? What are some possible outcomes for those who party 24/7 and continue with this behavior over time? Learn to be the CEO of your life and change course when necessary.

An analogy to think about is how successful companies periodically conduct what is known as strategic planning. Strategic planning is an exercise most executives participate in to review the company's progress and direction for the next few years. They evaluate strengths and weaknesses, research industry trends, and determine goals and action plans. This exercise shouldn't be reserved for businesses only; people should do their own strategic plans. Keep it simple. Maybe the next time you enjoy a cup of coffee, have a piece of paper and a pencil ready for you to reflect and write down your thoughts on the following areas:

Professional Life
- Where do I want to be in five years?
- How is the industry I am in changing?
- What skills are/will be needed?
- How am I doing today at work?
- Am I a top performer or have I been dropping the ball?

- What will likely happen if I continue with this behavior?
- What areas can I improve on?
- What actions can I take to improve on those areas?
- What does success look like for me?
- How do I scale my income?

As you answer these questions, if you find yourself to be unmotivated, perhaps you should consider another job or career. What career sounds more appealing to you? What technical and interpersonal skills do you need to get there? What actions can you take to move in that direction? Should you start your own business?

Financial Life:
- Is my financial situation getting better or worse over time?

By now you should have insight into your 3 KFIs and be able to answer this question easily. If it is getting better, what actions should I continue to take or should I start taking to reach my goals sooner? If it is getting worse, what happens if I continue on this trajectory? What can I do to change? What else should I be learning about it?

Feel free to expand on these types of questions to your family life, spiritual life, and health life if you desire. Most important is to write down 1 to 3 goals you will start working on immediately. Recall that your goals should be specific, measurable, attainable, relevant, and timetabled. Repeat this exercise once a year. Let me share an example of how this type of thinking led me to a promotion at work.

I started as a junior consultant working at a large multinational corporation in Oregon. The first few days were very challenging. My job was to develop complex computer models of their global operations and help them find ways to save money and improve service. I was dealing with dozens of datasets and was very slow to manipulate them into the computer model I needed to build. I observed that the senior consultants at my company did not struggle as much as I did and were all very proficient in Structured Query Language (SQL). SQL is code to communicate with databases. I observed that knowledge of SQL made a big difference in relation to how fast a consultant could turn around a project. After 3 months in the job, I concluded that I didn't lack the necessary business knowledge to do the job. However, I was a laggard from a technical skills perspective.

So, what did I do?

I researched and read a $10 book on how to get started with SQL. I applied what I learned immediately to my second project. The gains in productivity were noticeable, and by the end of my first year at work, I was being considered for a promotion to senior consultant. This experience also taught me that it is important to show improvement first, and then consistently deliver your work at a higher level before your boss or company feels confident to promote you. This promotion resulted in an annual salary increase of $10,000. At the time, it felt like I had won the lottery. To this day, I believe that a $10 SQL book has been one of my best investments.

Know that your pay comes from the exchange of something of value for money. This something of value is known as your work. Whether you are an employee or an entrepreneur, you are compensated for solving problems, providing value, and delighting customers. Therefore, the more valuable your work is, the more money you will make in the long-term.

Let's discuss some ways you can realize significant improvements to your career and financial life.

Besides taking stock and reflecting on your current situation, speak with people who are more successful than you are in the area you are trying to improve. Establish a periodic conversation with a person who is a mentor to you or someone you admire professionally. You can do this in person over a meal or coffee, or perhaps even remotely by phone or virtual conferencing. Ask questions about what actions the person took to be where they are, share your goals and plans, and ask for their feedback. Approach this relationship as a two-way street, like a friendship; otherwise, you may strain the relationship. If you can't think of anyone who could be a good mentor to you, leverage professional social media to find people. Set up a LinkedIn account to network and follow other professionals. LinkedIn is also helpful for those looking for a job. Jobs are posted daily, and you can also gain insights on salary ranges and have direct access to many recruiters. Follow these steps and grow your professional network in an organic healthy way.

Returning to the point of speaking with successful professionals, dedicate time to learn and address any gaps you identify in your skills. This should give you a roadmap of items you should work on. There are many educational resources you can find online for free to help you learn. However, remember that books are also great and typically very cheap or free. Visit your local library to borrow books that can help you with your career.

I've been focused so far in this chapter on helping you gain insight on how to improve your ability to make money within your job or career. Another area you should strive to improve on is in your knowledge of investments. We've only touched on the surface of the topics of investments; however, it is up to you to continue learning and becoming more educated on how investments work and what should you do about it.

Start by establishing a relationship with a licensed financial advisor who will spend the time to educate you on different financial instruments and teach you how to leverage them in your personal financial life. Ask the professional if he or she is a fiduciary advisor. Preferably, you'd want to work with a fiduciary advisor. A fiduciary duty requires the highest standard of care, meaning that the advisor should always act in your best interest. This could save you from running into advisors who are more interested in selling you an expensive product you don't need. If possible, establish a relationship with more than one professional so you have different points of view to balance. Finally, read more investment books to boost your knowledge even further. Start with books on the topics of stocks and real estate, and branch out from there. If you don't read books today, that is a habit you should pick as soon as possible. Start small, and shoot for 15 minutes of reading in the mornings or at a time that is convenient for you. If reading is not an option for you, try audiobooks or podcasts. Make it a priority in your life. You may find out that what you read can completely change and improve how you see the world. Never stop learning.

In conclusion, I strongly believe you will improve your financial condition if you follow the moves I've outlined here in this book. Digitize and visualize your money, get your financial priorities right, shrink today and expand your tomorrow, invest now for your future, and have a long-term growth action plan. Know that the race to wealth is typically long. It's okay to make mistakes and have ups and downs. Most importantly, keep an eye on your long-term trajectory and correct it when you need to. I close this book with one last quote:

"It's hard to beat a person who never gives up."

Babe Ruth

MOVE 5: HAVE A LONG-TERM GROWTH ACTION PLAN

Key Action Items
Visit **rebrand.ly/MoneyMoves** for more resources.

1. Take stock of where you are today; are you productive?
2. Reflect on your professional and financial lives. What are the gaps? What are you doing about them? Establish 1 to 3 goals to work on. Repeat this exercise yearly.
3. Establish a connection and get feedback from a successful professional or mentor.
4. Act on developing your skills. Take a course, read a book, listen to a podcast, etc.
5. Connect with 1 or more financial advisors. Find a fiduciary advisor if possible. Ask them to explain investment options to you.

Read investment-specific books on your own. See the link above for recommendations.

INDEX

4

4 financial walls, 14, 17
401(k), 37, 48
403(b), 48

5

529, 57

A

assets, 8, 9, 19, 47, 49, 50, 51, 56

B

basic needs, 17, 18, 37
bonds, 3, 49, 50, 56
budget, 6, 14, 15, 16, 32, 34, 38, 55, 60

C

capital gains, 50, 57
car, 8, 15, 18, 19, 36, 39, 55
carpe diem, 63
CD, 27
checking, 27
compounding, 47, 54
credit card, 2, 7, 8, 30, 39
credit score, 6, 10, 12, 35, 55

D

debt, 2, 9, 10, 14, 15, 16, 21, 27, 28, 31, 33, 35, 36, 37, 38, 40, 41, 42, 45, 46, 47, 54, 56, 57, 75
Debt collectors, 41
debts, 8, 9, 10, 12, 15, 32, 35, 40, 42, 44, 47, 55
disability, 24
diversification, 50, 51
dividend, 50
Dow Jones Industrial Average, 51
down payment, 15, 16, 55, 56

E

emergency fund, 14, 18, 26, 27, 35, 37, 38, 42, 55, 56, 57
ESA, 57
estate planning, 26
Exchange-traded funds, 51

F

Fair Debt Collection Practices Act, 41
fiduciary advisor, 69, 71
financial advisor, 16, 17, 68

H

HSA, 58

I

Identity theft, 24
Individual Retirement Accounts, 52
insurance, 14, 15, 16, 17, 18, 19,

20, 21, 22, 23, 24, 25, 26, 28
investments, iii, 3, 6, 14, 15, 23, 28, 34, 35, 37, 38, 43, 45, 46, 47, 51, 53, 59, 67, 68
IRS, 15, 49, 52, 58, 59

K

key financial indicators, 8, 35
KFI, 8, 10, 55

L

liabilities, 8

M

Maslow's hierarchy of needs, 17
Medicaid, 25
Medicare, 25
mentor, 16, 17, 67, 71
money market, 27
money shield, 14, 15, 16, 18, 26, 28, 32, 35, 37, 42, 43, 44, 45
mutual fund, 51

N

net income, 8, 9, 12, 31, 35, 42
net worth, 8, 9, 12, 31, 35, 42, 54

O

online financial platform, 6, 9, 10

P

Pareto Principle, 34
post-tax, 48
pre-tax, 48, 58

R

real estate, 31, 50, 56, 69
retirement, 3, 7, 14, 15, 35, 37, 38, 42, 43, 46, 47, 48, 50, 51, 52, 53, 54, 56, 57, 59
Roth 401(k), 48
Roth 403(b), 48

S

S&P 500, 45, 51
S.M.A.R.T, 33
savings, 21, 22, 23, 26, 27, 32, 33, 38, 42, 43, 57, 60
social security, 24, 25
stocks, 8, 49, 50, 51, 56, 69
strategic planning, 64

T

tax-deferred, 22, 48, 52
tax-free, 22, 48, 52, 57, 58

ABOUT THE AUTHOR

A first-generation American, Lucas paid off $33,000 in student debt while in his twenties. He accomplished this milestone in less than 18 months after graduate school at the end of the Great Recession. Lucas immigrated to the United States at the young age of 17 and learned how to win with his finances through a combination of his educational background in business and his research on the topic. Lucas developed a practical framework to get out of debt, and then thrive financially regardless of economic conditions. This book captures his learnings and teachings on how the average person can start winning with money and achieve financial security.

Made in the USA
Coppell, TX
26 April 2022